LEARNING GUIDE

Contents

How to Use This Guide

This Learning Guide for *Teaching and Learning with Technology, Third Edition*, provides you with diverse opportunities to reinforce and expand upon the knowledge and experiences gained from the textbook. Use these activities to review and apply chapter content, deepen your understanding of key concepts, and connect educational technology topics to real world teaching experiences.

Organization

The Learning Guide begins with a Course Pre-Test. Taking this test will help you to determine your current level of understanding of course content. The Learning Guide culminates in a Course Post-Test. Taking the Post-Test offers you an opportunity to demonstrate for yourself the mastery of content that you have achieved.

The Learning Guide is organized into a series of chapter-specific activities and activities that encompass multiple chapter concepts. The chapter-specific activities include:

1. Projects, both individual and group, to apply the knowledge obtained in each chapter
2. Reflections that will encourage deeper understanding of the topics discussed
3. Puzzles to review and practice key terms
4. Video Review Guides related to the collection of classroom videos keyed to the text that are available in MyLabSchool. These videos are windows into real classrooms in action and the guides will help you to discern the critical points that reinforce and relate to chapter content

Multi-chapter activities integrate the concepts and examples from several chapters into broader critical thinking experiences. These activities include Problem-Based Learning Activities and Field Experience Activities for those students for whom field work is a component of their educational technology course. These activities offer opportunities for group problem solving and for the application of educational technology concepts to real-world classrooms.

For the Faculty

The Instructor Resource Center (www.ablongman.com/irc) provides answer keys for the Puzzles, Video Reviews, and Problem-Based Learning Scenarios for assessment. You can register to secure access to this web site, or contact your Allyn and Bacon sales representative.

Learning Guide

for

Lever-Duffy and McDonald

Teaching and Learning with Technology

Third Edition

prepared by

Ana Ciereszko
Miami Dade College

Judy Lever-Duffy
Miami Dade College

PEARSON

Boston   New York   San Francisco
Mexico City   Montreal   Toronto   London   Madrid   Munich   Paris
Hong Kong   Singapore   Tokyo   Cape Town   Sydney

ISBN-13: 978-0-205-54890-3
ISBN-10:   0-205-54890-3

Printed in the United States of America

10 9 8 7 6 5 4 3 2 1   11 10 09 08 07

Pre-test: Complete the following to determine your pre-course level of educational technology competency. Circle the best answer from the choices

1. The broadest definition of educational technology today typically includes:
    A. Primarily audio and visual media
    B. Print, models, and manipulatives
    C. Only digital media
    D. All types of learning resources systems and media

2. A theorist that is well known for seeing learning from a behaviorist perspective is:
    A. B. F. Skinner
    B. Howard Gardner
    C. Jean Piaget
    D. Lev Vygotsky

3. Performance objectives are objectives that specify what the learner will be able to do when the instructional event concludes.   A. True   B. False

4. Bloom's Taxonomy levels relate to categories of cognition. These levels are equivalent in difficulty and in usefulness in the learning process.   A. True   B. False

5. Which of the following is NOT an input device in a computer?
    A. keyboard
    B. touchpad
    C. printer
    D. mouse

6. Hard disks are the best storage device for programs and documents, because they hardly ever break down.   A. True   B. False

7. When determining which new classroom equipment to select, such as a printer, scanner, monitor, projector, or any other digital device, it is important to consider the ease of setup, ease of use, and how much space it will occupy in the classroom.   A. True   B. False

8. If one needs to project an image from a computer onto a screen, one would select a:
    A. webcam
    B. PDA
    C. scanner
    D. data projector

9. Classroom management software is often used to prepare handouts and worksheets for students.   A. True   B. False

10. Software that is used to organize and track information, such as listing academic resources, is known as:
    A. word processing
    B. spreadsheets
    C. database management
    D. presentation

11. Software that is designed to reinforce previously presented content is known as:
    A. drill-and-practice
    B. concept mapping software
    C. simulations
    D. educational games

12. Software that allows for visual brainstorming is called authoring software.
    A. True   B. False

1

13. To synchronously connect two or more classrooms or locations, one would use an Internet tool called
   A. portal
   B. videoconferencing
   C. search engine
   D. streaming video

14. A uniform resource collector (URL) is used to find an individual's email address.
   A. True   B. False

15. It is better to use a PDF file rather than an HTML file because a PDF file cannot be edited by the user and maintains its format.
   A. True   B. False

16. Which of the following may NOT be appropriate to use as you conduct research for a term paper?
   A. blog
   B. online encyclopedia
   C. portal
   D. online publication

17. Optical media includes CDs, DVDs, and MP3 files.   A. True   B. False

18. Which of the following is NOT used to display video technologies?
   A. scanner
   B. digital projectors
   C. TV monitors
   D. computer monitor

19. Transmission of video within a school is often done via:
   A. broadcast video
   B. ITFS (Instructional Television Fixed Service)
   C. CCTV (closed–circuit TV)
   D. cablecast

20. A disadvantage of distance education is that students can only learn from reading text, since there is no video or audio available.   A. True   B. False

21. Teachers who teach online must be concerned about:
   A. students' readiness to learn within a new environment
   B. the availability of the appropriate technologies to deliver instruction
   C. providing alternative modes when the technology malfunctions or fails
   D. all of the above

22. Fair use refers to how copyrighted material may be used in face-to-face instruction.
   A. True   B. False

23. The ability of using computers to create a real or imagined three-dimensional place is called:
   A. convergence
   B. digitalization
   C. virtual reality
   D. artificial intelligence

24. The No Child Left Behind (NCLB) Act does NOT address educational technology literacy standards.   A. True   B. False

25. NETS-T refers to the National Educational Technology Standards for:
   A. teachers
   B. students
   C. technology trainers
   D. administrators

CHAPTER 1
PROJECT 1
EDUCATIONAL TECHNOLOGY AND ME

In 1-2 word processed pages, describe any experience you have in teaching or helping in schools; what you have seen as a teacher or student in the use of technology in K12 classrooms; and finally, how you feel technology should be integrated into teaching and learning. You should address the following questions in your essay:

- How would you define educational technology?
- What is its role in teaching? In learning?
- What factors encourage or discourage the use of technology in the classroom?

CHAPTER 1
PROJECT 2
LEARNING THEORIES AND EDUCATIONAL TECHNOLOGY

Research learning theories and then create a table using a format similar to the one below. You must include all theories and theorists mentioned in the text *AND AT LEAST ONE ADDITIONAL THEORIST* for each theoretical perspective from research on the Internet. You may also include any other theories you discover in your research.

Theory	Key Theorists	Summary of Theory	What role might technology play when implementing this theory in the classroom?
Behaviorist			
Cognitivist			
Constructivist			
Multiple Intelligences			
Learning Styles			
Other			

CHAPTER 1—FOR REFLECTION

1. Identify a favorite teacher in elementary or secondary school. Describe three practices or techniques that this teacher employed to meet your own learning needs that were significant in helping you learn.

2. Using Howard Gardner's theory of multiple intelligences, describe three intelligences in which you excel and give an example of each. How could these intelligences be useful when you become a teacher?

3. Assess your own technology skills and list three areas in which you could improve your abilities. How would you go about improving in these areas?

CHAPTER 1 PUZZLER

www.CrosswordWeaver.com

CHAPTER 1 PUZZLER CLUES

ACROSS

1 looking at the same thing and seeing it in different ways
4 _____ style - preferences individuals have as to how best to receive information
5 one of the most well-known behaviorists
8 _____ style - how each person's tendencies and preferences affect the learning process
10 their primary responsibility is the management of educational technology equipment
12 believe learning is a mental operation that takes place when information enters through the senses, undergoes mental manipulation, is stored and finally used.
14 includes printed paper, models project and nonprojected visuals, as well as digital audio and video
18 those who believe that learning is essentially a passive process, that one learns as a response to the environment, rather than through mental activity
21 the inherent capability of the learner to understand and learn
23 a constructivist who described four major states of development in children
24 behaviorists see learning as this (hint: two words separated by a hyphen)

DOWN

1 a constructivist who adapted Piaget's perspective and applied it to children using technology
2 believe knowledge is a unique product for each individual resulting from the learning process
3 _____ style - affected by a teacher's learning style, cognitive style and dominant intelligence
6 _____ cycle - checking feedback from learner to assure that accurate communication has taken place
7 a type of instruction developed in the 1950's where a series of small steps required immediate responses from the learner
9 _____ factors - those that may interfere with communication such as loud noise, interruptions, dim lighting, and uncomfortable temperatures
11 _____ event - where knowledge and skills are transferred from teacher to students
13 federally funded initiative to develop standards for technology for both teachers and students
15 obtaining confirmation from receiver that information was accurately received
16 an instrument to measure cognitive style
17 developed the theory of multiple intelligences
19 includes personal values, cultural heritage and social belief system
20 association that has been prominent in the area of design and implementation of educational technology for the past seventy-five years
22 intelligence quotient

CHAPTER 1 VIDEO REVIEW GUIDE

The following questions relate to the videos designated in the margins of chapter 1. Videos are available in MyLabSchool (www.mylabschool.com. Go to Courses/ appropriate course/Video Lab or use the Assignment ID).

Video: *Strategies for Teaching Diverse Learners*
(Educational Psychology, Individual Differences, Assignment ID EPV2)

"Strategies for Teaching Diverse Learners" describes how to apply the theory of multiple intelligences to meet the needs of diverse learners by providing differentiated instruction. After viewing the video, respond to the following:

1. List two things the teacher believes she needs to know about her students to be able to provide different ways of teaching them.

2. Give specific examples of how these two teachers are using the theory of multiple intelligences as they give students assignments.

3. Suggest two other activities that these teachers could have assigned their students to engage their multiple intelligences.

Video: *Multiple Intelligences in the Classroom*
(Educational Psychology, Individual Differences, Assignment ID EPV2)

This video explains Howard Gardner's Theory of Multiple Intelligences and ways in which it may be incorporated into instruction. After viewing the video, respond to the following:

1. Six different centers based on Gardner's multiple intelligences were created in the classroom. How were students selected to attend the different centers?

2. What was the major concern the teacher had regarding the students' choice and how was it resolved?

3. List five of the types of intelligences that, according to Howard Gardner, every person possesses.

4. How can technology help to address the diverse intelligences you are likely to find in your classroom?

CHAPTER 2
PROJECT 1
PERFORMANCE OBJECTIVE PRACTICE

This project is an opportunity for you to practice writing performance objectives.
Write a performance objective for a content area and/or grade level of your choice for
EACH of the cognitive domains below. Share your objectives with one or two of your
peers and assist each other in fine-tuning your objectives so that they meet
performance objectives criteria discussed in class.

KNOWLEDGE LEVEL
(bringing appropriate material to mind)
COMPREHENSION LEVEL
(understanding material and using it without relating it to other material)
APPLICATION LEVEL
(using material learned to apply to other concepts)
ANALYSIS LEVEL
(breaking material down into its parts to clarify it)
EVALUATION LEVEL
(judging the value of material)
SYNTHESIS LEVEL
(putting together parts into a whole)

CHAPTER 2
PROJECT 2
LESSON PLANNING INTERVIEW

This project is designed to engage you in the practice of talking to teachers about
teaching methods and support media in order to help you develop your own ideas
about how to teach in your own classroom. As you gain classroom experience, your
ability to create good lesson plans will improve. The best teachers are always looking
for and finding ways to improve teaching and learning.

Interview a teacher about how s/he develops, evaluates, and modifies his or her own
lesson plans and teaching methods. Compare your notes of the planning process
with the steps of the DID model. In 1-2 pages, describe the methods used by the
teacher and identify their strengths and weaknesses when compared to the DID
model.
- *Be sure to inquire what technologies are used to support the instruction and why
  that particular technology was selected.*
- *Include the teacher's name, grade level, and school*

CHAPTER 2—FOR REFLECTION

1. Using the DID Steps (see Table 2.1 in the textbook), identify which step will be the hardest for you to complete and why. Describe ways in which you can overcome this difficulty to become a successful teacher.

2. Think back on a classroom environment in which you were not as successful as you might have wanted to be. Identify whether it was the physical space, the classroom climate or the attitudes you encountered from the teacher and/or other students that may have hindered your learning.

3. This chapter described how proper planning ensures success in teaching and learning. Describe two activities (not educational in nature) in which you have been involved in the past which were NOT successful due to lack of planning.

 **LEARNING GUIDE**

CHAPTER 2 PUZZLER

CHAPTER 2 PUZZLER CLUES

ACROSS

1 a system which includes three planning processes to maximize the quality of teaching (three words connected by hyphens)

7 the actions and activities that a teacher uses to communicate a concept

9 _____ phase - that which articulates all the broad steps that must be taken to ensure that instruction occurs as conceived

10 the lowest level in Bloom's taxonomy

12 pedagogical _____ - a sequence of specific methods that promote and support effective instruction

15 the technologies that are used to facilitate a method of teaching

17 the _____ instructional design (DID) model that may be used to build effective instruction

18 the principles and methods of instruction

21 a performance _____ specifies what the learner will be able to do at the end of an instructional event

22 learning _____ includes all the conditions, circumstances and influences that affect the learner's development

23 _____ design model - a fully articulated design template to help educators in the first phase of planning to help them visualize their planned instruction holistically, as an entire unit

24 educator who created a model that is part of the foundation for today's instructional design systems

DOWN

2 _____ instruction - that which has been thoroughly thought out and articulated by a skillful and creative educator

3 _____ phase - where the unit is broken down into daily lesson plans

4 Bloom's _____ categorizes levels of thinking

5 _____ loop is used during every step of the process for midcourse corrections

6 _____ strategies are the methods used by the instructor to assist students in achieving the objectives

8 _____ feedback - occurs at the end of a process to help revise each step and serves as a final check

11 theorists who led the effort to identify categories of cognition

13 the highest level in Bloom's taxonomy

14 _____ strategies are the techniques and activities students must engage in, in order to master the content

16 _____ approach - a carefully planned, step-by-step process to design, create, evaluate and revise instruction

18 lesson _____ is the practical product of the instructional design product

19 _____ feedback - ensures the continuous flow of information so that corrections and adjustments can be made during the process

20 instructional _____ plan (IAP) helps to articulate a lesson's to-do list

CHAPTER 2 VIDEO REVIEW GUIDE

The following questions relate to the videos designated in the margins of chapter 2. Videos are available in My Lab School (www.mylabschool.com. Go to Courses/ Educational Technology/Video Lab or use the Assignment ID).

Video: *Learning the Rules for Computer Use*
(Educational Technology, Planning Technology-Enhanced Instruction, Assignment ID ETV1)

In *"Learning the Rules for Computer Use"* a set of rules for computer usage is presented to assist in classroom management.

1. What are two problems that the teacher identified as she prepared to use computers in the classroom?

2. How were these challenges overcome?

3. List the essential components of a lesson plan. Which step of the lesson plan is depicted in this video?

Video: *Using Technology to Meet Objectives*
(Educational Technology, The New Realities of Teaching, Assignment ID ETV5)

A kindergarten class learns how to use KidPix on computers to teach math, technology and English as a Second Language objectives. After viewing the video, respond to the following:

1. Was the technology used in this lesson appropriate for the concepts being taught?

2. Give examples of how the teacher was meeting the diverse needs of her students.

3. Construct two performance objectives that may have been written for the lesson observed in this video.

CHAPTER 3
PROJECT 1
BUYING A COMPUTER

In this project you will have an opportunity to consider what kind of computer you would like for your classroom.

Imagine this scenario . . .

Your school has allocated enough money for each teacher to buy a computer for their classroom. You have been selected to represent your grade level or subject area to serve on the committee that decides what features these classroom computers should have. Research a computer system and decide what you are going to suggest the committee buys. For each component you feel is important, justify your suggestion and relate that component to why you need it to better use this computer in the classroom. Prepare a 1-2 page word-processed explanation of your recommendation that you feel would convince the committee of the benefits of your suggestions.

Be specific and realistic. You may use local retail prices or (the usually lower) prices from online or mail order sales. Be sure you explain why you think configuring a computer with a specific option will benefit teachers or students. You might like to organize the features you recommend in a table.

CHAPTER 3
PROJECT 2
COMPUTER BASICS HANDOUT

This project helps you to focus on the essential computer concepts both you and your students need to master. Using the computer concepts you have learned from this chapter, create a Computer Basics handout that teaches key computer concepts to the grade level you would like to teach. The handout should be word-processed and include clip art or illustrations from the text's companion web site or from other sources. Print out a hard copy of the handout to turn in.

- *Even the youngest children can be introduced to computers. Be creative in teaching these skills and ideas to younger children by using a constructivist approach that bridges what they currently know to these new ideas.*
- *Be sure font, vocabulary, and graphics are suitable for the grade level the handout is designed for.*

CHAPTER 3—FOR REFLECTION

1. Describe your memories of the first time you used a computer. How old were you, in what setting did it occur (at home, in school, at work)? Did you feel intimidated by it or was it a new, fun challenge for you? What made it a fearful or pleasant experience?

2. If there were no outside influences, such as school or work, requiring you to use computers, would you choose to use them? Why or why not?

3. Reflect on how computers affect your life. List three ways in which your life is different because of computers.

CHAPTER 3 PUZZLER

www.CrosswordWeaver.com

CHAPTER 3 PUZZLER CLUES

ACROSS

1 computer _____ - includes the collection of computer hardware
3 a program written specifically to disrupt computer operations or to destroy data
10 _____ device - any piece of hardware that moves information out of the computer
12 computer components that are physical in nature and, therefore, can be touched
14 the amount of data that is roughly equal to one alphabetic or numeric character
15 establishes the method of interaction between the user and the computer
18 abbreviation for a smaller network that connects machines in a local area, such as a classroom or a school
20 small graphic that represents one of the system's options
22 tiny silicon slices containing millions of electronic circuits
23 ____ copy - the printed form of the information generated in the computer
26 a newer type of monitor screen, also used in laptops
27 list of command options that appears across the top of the program window
28 "read only memory" chips in which only the BIOS is stored
29 _____ copy - electronic form, such as seen on the computer monitor
30 _____ device - includes any computer peripheral that might be used to enter data into the computer
32 abbreviation for a large network that connects machines across a wide area
33 ____ up - to duplicate computer files in case the hard drive crashes
34 temporary electronic storage used by the computer to complete tasks
35 one of the most popular operating systems
36 a digital organizer that one creates to hold related files
37 a small unit of data that is sent through the network to try to speed up the transmission process

DOWN

2 another term for programs written in a special language that tells a computer how to accomplish a task
4 refers to the clarity and crispness of the images on a monitor
5 permanent electronic space where the computer stores instructions and data that it will use later
6 a pointing device that rolls, usually on a special pad, on the desk
7 the carrying capacity of the transmission media for sending information in a network
8 "picture element", a single colored dot that when combined with other dots forms an image
9 _____ program - improves or monitors computer operations
11 a special piece of equipment that is the centralized connection for a network
13 a more powerful computer that provides services to all computers in a network
16 computing _____ - the steps of taking in data, processing it, storing it and outputting results
17 hard ____ - the most common storage device because of its large capacity
19 any workstation or peripheral that is connected to the network

CHAPTER 3 VIDEO REVIEW GUIDE

The following questions relate to the videos designated in the margins of chapter 3. Videos are available in My Lab School (www.mylabschool.com. Go to Courses/ Educational Technology/Video Lab or use the Assignment ID).

Video: *Managing Technology in the Classroom*
(Educational Technology, Planning Technology-Enhanced Instruction, Assignment ID ETV1)

This video demonstrates how technology may be used to support and enhance instruction, as well as the importance of developing an "acceptable use" policy.

1. This video suggests several ways that technology may be used in schools to enhance instruction. List two of them.

2. The video discusses the need for an "acceptable use" policy. Why is that and how is this policy conveyed to students?

3. How does the video address parents' concerns about misuse of the Internet?

4. Imagine what classrooms will be like twenty years from now. Do you think that the technology will reduce the need for, or even replace, teachers?

Video: *An Adaptive Keyboard*
(Educational Technology, Priority: Technology and Inclusion, Assignment ID ETV23)

In this video, a special needs student is shown using an adaptive keyboard in the classroom.

1. Describe how the adaptive keyboard may be used to assist in instruction.

2. As a result of watching this video, how has your view of the role of technology for students with special needs changed?

3. Use the Internet to research other input and output devices that may be used to assist special needs students.

CHAPTER 4
PROJECT 1
TECHNOLOGY BUDGET

Imagine this scenario . . .

Because of your demonstrated teaching skill and technological knowledge, you have just been awarded $20,000 to spend on computer technology (including accessories) for your classroom. How will you spend this money? For each item, describe what you will purchase and how many. Culminate with an essay explaining how will you use these items in your classroom?
- Be specific and realistic. List quantities, specific items and prices. You may use local retail prices or (the usually lower) prices from online or mail order sales.
- You might like to set up the budget in a word-processing table: item, quantity, price, etc. (or in an electronic spreadsheet).

CHAPTER 4
PROJECT 2
CREATING A DIGITAL PHOTO ESSAY

Create an educational digital photo essay on a topic of your choice for the grade level you would like to teach. Obtain 10-15 digital images for your essay by:
- Using a digital still camera or digital video camera (taking still images)
- Shoot images via photographic film and have the prints processed on a photo CD-ROM

Shoot images via photographic film and then scan the prints on a flatbed scanner. Then, insert the images into any word-processed document or into a PowerPoint presentation. Print out your photo essay and attach it to a 1-2 page word processed document in which you explain how you might use this photo essay in your classroom. If you insert the images into PowerPoint, print the essay as a 2 slides per page handout.

CHAPTER 4—FOR REFLECTION

1. When selecting new classroom equipment, there are several important considerations, such as ease of setup, ease of use, and whether tutorials are available. Are these more or less important to you than the monetary cost of the equipment? Explain why or why not?

2. How many of the digital technologies discussed in this chapter have you used? Have you used them in an educational setting or elsewhere?

3. Try to recall two or three disabled individuals that you have met in the past. How could the digital technologies described in this chapter have been used or adapted to help these disabled individuals?

CHAPTER 4 PUZZLER

www.CrosswordWeaver.com

CHAPTER 4 PUZZLER CLUES

ACROSS

3 scan _____ - transforms a computer's image into one that can be displayed through analog technology such as a TV monitor
5 hardware that is connected to the computer system
7 _____ screen - a special light-sensitive screen that accepts commands by interpreting interruptions to light on a specific spot of the screen
9 _____ tablet - an electronic pad with a stylus that allows one to draw or create artwork
10 _____ PC - similar to a laptop computer but one is able to 'write' on the screen with a stylus
11 _____ camera - works like a traditional camera but does not use film; photos are stored in a memory card
12 this device uses a stylus to input handwritten information to select commands and may also 'write' by using predetermined written symbols, called gestures
15 _____ devices - technology that does not need to be connected via a wire
18 a type of audio output that is used by one individual and does not disturb others
19 _____ scanner - works like a personal copier, duplicates whatever is placed on it (there is a hyphen separating two words)
20 _____ technology - enables a computer to accept verbal commands
21 points of connection between a computer system and its peripherals
24 data _____ - this device can display images from a computer system or from a video source
25 electronic _____ - this device allows you to store what has been written on the display surface

DOWN

1 _____ reality - combination of hardware and software that together create an interactive environment
2 _____ card - stores data, often used in digital cameras
4 electronic version of a popular reading device (hint: has a hyphen)
6 another name for a graphic tablet because they convert lines into their digital equivalents
8 _____ computers - small devices that can handle personal information as well as abbreviated versions of popular software
13 one of the most common input devices
14 audio output devices, they transmit sound
16 an input device that captures and then translates printed copy into digital data
17 a digital camera usually set up on top of the monitor to capture images for communication via the Internet
22 a high-speed port found on newer computers (abbreviation)
23 _____ software - this type of software recognizes printed characters and turns them into their word-processing equivalent

CHAPTER 4 VIDEO REVIEW GUIDE

The following questions relate to the videos designated in the margins of chapter 4. Videos are available in My Lab School (www.mylabschool.com. Go to Courses/ Educational Technology/Video Lab or use the Assignment ID).

Video: *Teaching Content with Technology*
(Educational Technology, Teaching Content with Technology, Assignment ID ETV18)

Several different technology activities such as Internet research, digital cameras and PowerPoint are integrated into a geometry lesson in a math methods course.

1. In this math methods course students are exploring tessellations (repeated patterns found in such things as bricks, tiles, etc.). They explore this concept through various formats. List two of the formats they used.

2. The professor commented on the need to evaluate lesson plans found on the Internet. What criteria is she using to evaluate these lesson plans?

3. How does the Internet help K-12 students on a day-to-day basis?

4. The Design-Plan-Act! (D-P-A) system includes three planning processes. Explain how these students, preparing to become teachers, were organizing their lessons.

Video: *Teaching with Wireless Devices*
(Educational Technology, Integrating Palm Pilots, Assignment ID ETV22)

Handheld computers, which were originally developed for the business world, are used in a fifth-grade classroom to reinforce math and language arts skills. These handheld computers contain abbreviated versions of productivity software such as word processing and spreadsheets, as well as games and educational software.

1. Describe three ways that handheld computers are used in this fifth-grade class to cover the curriculum.

2. Name three advantages of using handheld computers over desktops.

Video: *Using Handhelds in the Classroom*
(Educational Technology, Integrating Palm Pilots, Assignment ID ETV22)

In this video fifth-grade students help a graduate class of teachers to integrate handhelds into their teaching. The graduate students are experimenting with new ways to teach different aspects of the curriculum.

1. Describe three ways that graduate students (teachers) plan to use handheld computers to teach.

2. Name an important advantage, as described by Professor Topp, of handhelds over laptop computers.

3. Identify general advantages of wireless technology in the classroom.

CHAPTER 5
PROJECT 1
TEACHER INTERVIEW

In this project you will interview a teacher to discover the types of productivity software he or she uses either for administrative tasks or for academic activities. Select a teacher at a school near you. Ask your interviewee to explain how and why he or she chooses software packages for the classroom tasks at hand. Also inquire as to the success of the applications selected and any shortcomings encountered. In 1-2 pages, report your interview in a question and answer format. Add your own summary paragraphs detailing how your view of the application of productivity software to education has or has not been changed as a result of what you learned from the interview.

- Include the name and school of your interviewee.
- Be sure to be on time for the interview. Have your questions ready and take accurate notes. You may wish to tape record the interview but be sure to get your interviewee's permission first.

CHAPTER 5
PROJECT 2
APPLICATIONS RESEARCH

One of the best ways to get new teaching ideas is to discover what your colleagues are doing. For this project, use the Internet to find an innovative educational application for EACH of the productivity software packages. After reading the ideas, create and complete a table like the one below to share with your peers.

Application	URL of site	Age/Grade	Description of Application
Word Processing			
Electronic Spreadsheets			
Data Base Management			
Presentation Software			

Be sure to look for sites that have some authority such as those that are maintained by educational organizations, universities, and state or local school districts.

CHAPTER 5—FOR REFLECTION

1. As a student, you have probably received grades in different formats. Long ago, you probably received report cards on paper, perhaps even handwritten. Nowadays, many report cards are online, accessible to students and parents soon after the grades are input. What do you think are the advantages and disadvantages of each approach? Please answer this question as if you were a parent and also as a teacher.

2. When you look at a document such as an assignment or worksheet, is it important to you how it is laid out, how easy it is to read, whether it has graphics or not? Do you think it is important to students? Why or why not?

3. Recall a class where presentation software, such as PowerPoint, was used. Did you enjoy the experience? Was it easy to take notes? Did you stay focused on the presentation, or did your attention drift into other thoughts? Could the presentation have been modified to make it more interactive, more interesting? How?

CHAPTER 5 PUZZLER

CHAPTER 5 PUZZLER CLUES

ACROSS

3 documents that are pre-formatted for a specific use but contain no data

6 what-if _____ is used in electronic spreadsheets to predict how a certain change will affect other data

8 classroom _____ software - usually customized software written for educators to help manage school and classroom tasks

9 provides for customized output through the selection of specific records based on predefined criteria

10 software that is offered to users for a small fee or for a limited time

13 _____ software assists educators and students in the teaching and learning process

14 _____ software - generic business-application software that may be adapted for educators to use for administrative and professional tasks

15 _____ productivity package combines or bundles several software applications into one unit

16 _____-checking ensures that words in a document are written correctly

18 _____ art - ready-made artwork that can be inserted into a document

20 provides easy-to-use tools for visual displays of numeric data

21 a pre-made mathematical formula that is stored in a spreadsheet program

22 a mini-program that creates a customized template

23 _____ software - a well-known example of this software is PowerPoint

DOWN

1 software that is offered to users with no charge

2 _____ management software allows for data retrieval of customized records and the ability to organize reports from the data

4 a pre-recorded set of commands for a word processor that automates a complex task

5 a site _____ allows the use of a software package on all machines within an organization

7 an electronic _____ is used to organize, input, edit, and chart data

11 _____ software assists in accomplishing professional and management tasks

12 _____-_____ software has replaced the typewriter for text-oriented tasks (include hyphen in puzzle)

13 an inexpensive and easy way to store and access digital documents

14 _____ assessment software is an alternative method of tracking student progress

17 in word-processing this allows for changes to the look of a page, such as different fonts, margins, size of characters

19 multiple ways of accessing data to make it easy to comprehend

CHAPTER 5 VIDEO REVIEW GUIDE

The following questions relate to the videos designated in the margins of chapter 5. Videos are available in My Lab School (www.mylabschool.com. Go to Courses/ Educational Technology/Video Lab or use the Assignment ID).

Video: *Tools for Tracking Students*
(Educational Technology, Microsoft's Backyard, Assignment ID ETV26)

The Lake Washington School District received community funding for their technology initiatives. Among these initiatives is their online report card, which uses a web-based tool that allows students to be tracked over time. In addition, this tool provides for the storage of teacher lesson plans and gives meaningful assessment data to teachers and parents.

1. Discuss how this school district has been able to fund technology initiatives.

2. Describe how this classroom management software works.

3. List two advantages of using the software described in this video.

4. List possible problems with the implementation of this or other classroom management software.

Video: *Using PowerPoint*
(Educational Technology, Lewis and Clark Rediscovery, Assignment ID ETV12)

As part of a multi-state project to infuse technology in the classroom, middle school students are taught how to use PowerPoint. They then use this technology, as well as Inspiration software and Internet searches, to learn about the Lewis and Clark expedition.

1. Describe how this video shows the use of PowerPoint in the classroom.

2. What are some advantages of allowing students to learn by using technology?

Video: *Classroom Management Software*
(Educational Technology, Microsoft's Backyard, Assignment ID ETV26)

The Lake Washington School District developed a Class Server pilot project at one of its elementary schools. This online software – Class Server — allows teachers to create individualized assignments for their students. These assignments are aligned to standards and provide built-in assessments as well as immediate feedback to students and teachers.

1. Give two examples of how Class Server assists teachers.

2. How is Class Server similar to database management software?

3. Summarize the class management tools that Class Server offers to the district?

Video: *Digital Portfolios*
(Educational Technology, Digital Diagnostic Portfolios, Assignment ID ETV10)

Alverno College uses digital diagnostic portfolios in its teacher education program. These portfolios include student performance data, video clips, lessons plans, faculty feedback and self-assessment.

1. Give three advantages of using portfolio assessment, especially a digital portfolio, as demonstrated in this video.

2. Reflect on the material covered in Chapter 1 on diverse learners and explain how a digital portfolio assists in the assessment of students.

CHAPTER 6
PROJECT 1
SOFTWARE EVALUATION

In this project you will have the opportunity to practice reviewing academic software. Choose three software packages and complete the *Software Evaluation Rubric* for each package. The rubric can be found in your text and is downloadable from the companion web site at www.ablongman.com/lever-duffy3e. Be sure to note your evaluation of the program's strengths and weaknesses. After you complete the three evaluations, choose the software you like best and prepare a 1-2 page word-processed essay in which you describe how this software could be used to support instruction.

CHAPTER 6
PROJECT 2
CONCEPT MAPPING

This project gives you an opportunity to use and explore the application of concept mapping software. Go to the popular concept mapping software, Inspiration's, web site at www.inspiration.com and review the educator resources available there to become familiar with concept mapping. Then use Google to research the use of concept mapping software in the content area and/or grade level you plan to teach. Complete a table similar to the one below based upon your research. Include at least five possible activities that you might consider for your classroom that use either Inspiration or Kidspiration.

Grade	Content Area	Activity Description	How would you use this activity for Teaching or Learning?

Try creating your own concept map to teach a topic of your choice. If you need additional help becoming familiar with how to use Inspiration or Kidspiration, complete the Inspiration Skills Builder activity on the MyLabSchool site

CHAPTER 6—FOR REFLECTION

1. Imagine that you are teaching in a school. Select a grade level and subject matter and describe how you would use three different types of academic software to teach a specific topic.

2. Authoring systems include multimedia lessons using a hypermedia format, which allows each student to navigate through the program in a unique way. Do you think that you would have enjoyed learning by yourself using this format? Why or why not?

3. With so many academic resources available to teachers, it can be difficult to decide how and where they fit into instruction. Explain how you might utilize the many academic resources available to you during a typical day in your future classroom. Give specific examples.

CHAPTER 6 PUZZLER

CHAPTER 6 PUZZLER CLUES

ACROSS

2 _____ games provide students with the opportunity to solve mysteries and participate in other exciting activities

5 _____ programs are similar to paint programs but they create objects that can then be manipulated to create an image

8 _____ software presents new material in a carefully orchestrated instructional sequence with opportunities for practice and review

9 allows jumps to different web pages by a click of the mouse

10 software that presents the user with a model or situation in a computerized or virtual format

11 _____ software can be used to create, edit, or enhance digital images

17 _____ - _____software allows students to brainstorm the relationships among ideas (use hyphen)

20 _____ software allows students to move through the learning experience in their own unique way, jumping to different sections of the software depending on how they respond

21 _____ games exercise hand-eye coordination, reasoning and content practice

22 _____ programs allow one to create and manipulate digital pictures; they have a variety of brush and pen sizes and shapes

23 _____ learning systems (ILS) combine tutorials and drill-and-practice software as well as a classroom management support system

DOWN

1 _____-_____ software helps students acquire and practice skills that include forming and testing a hypothesis, and developing multiple-step strategies (include hyphen)

3 academic _____ allows for research on a specific area or discipline that provides reliable and authentic sources, usually through a subscription service

4 _____ software allows for storage of information that in the past was confined to the printed page (encyclopedias) with only a few pictures

6 _____ software allows you to alter or enhance an image, no matter how it was created

7 desktop _____ software allows the average computer user to create professional-looking printed or electronic material

12 _____ software may be used to enrich the teaching and learning environment

13 special _____ software is specialized to address the requirements of students with physical or learning impairments

14 _____ systems are used by educators to create their own instructional software

15 drill-and-_____ software is designed to reinforce previously presented content

16 _____ labs allow students to simulate laboratory experiments

17 _____ art images is ready-made artwork that can easily be added to other digital documents

18 educational _____ present and review instructional content in a fun, challenging way that engages students more that drill-and-practice or tutorial software

19 _____ software is used to convert hard-copy images to digital images

20 Hypertext Markup Language used on the Web and translated by Internet browsers into computer displays

CHAPTER 6 VIDEO REVIEW GUIDE

The following questions relate to the videos designated in the margins of chapter 6. Videos are available in My Lab School (www.mylabschool.com. Go to Courses/ Educational Technology/Video Lab or use the Assignment ID).

Video: *Using Authoring Software*
(Educational Technology, The Student Teaching Experience, Assignment ID ETV6)

HyperStudio, an authoring software, is highlighted in this video. Third-grade students are taught about Veteran's Day using this software.

1. What is the main use of HyperStudio in this video? What are some of the advantages as discussed by the teacher?

2. What properties of HyperStudio are NOT being used in this video?

3. What other software could have been used?

4. How was this lesson made interactive?

Video: *Drill and Practice*
(Educational Technology, Teaching Content with Technology, Assignment ID ETV18)

Drill and practice software is useful for learning that requires memorization and repetition. In this video, students use software to practice multiplication and the names of state capitals.

1. Describe drill and practice software.

2. What are some of the advantages AND disadvantages of drill and practice software?

Video: *Word Processing*
(Educational Technology, Priority: Technology and Inclusion, Assignment ID ETV23)

Word-processing can be used in many ways to enhance learning for students with special needs.

1. This video uses the term "social power" to explain benefits gained by special needs students when they learn to use the computer.

2. Describe three specific ways in which word-processing assists special needs students.

Video: *Using Concept Mapping Software*
(Educational Technology, Methods to Classroom, Assignment ID ETV19)

In this video we see how a teacher has managed to integrate technology into a classroom that has only two computers. We also see a student teacher use Inspiration, a type of concept mapping software, to help students organize their knowledge of the book they are reading in their social studies class.

1. How does this teacher effectively use one or two computers in a classroom?

2. How are students using concept mapping software (in this case, Inspiration) to learn social studies?

3. Concept mapping software is useful to teachers who subscribe to a particular learning theory. Which learning theory is that and why?

Video: *Virtual Chemistry Labs*
(Educational Technology, Virtual Chem Lab, Assignment ID ETV27)

Simulations are very effective in teaching students laboratory skills, especially in more advanced curriculum where the equipment and chemicals may not be available in the high school.

1. List three advantages of using simulations in a chemistry lab.

2. Should simulation software replace all real experiences (in this case, actual laboratory work)?

Video: *Using GIS Software*
(Educational Technology, GIS, Assignment ID ETV16)

Geographic Information Systems (GIS) is used to motivate students in two high school multidiscipline classes. GIS is used to analyze map-based data and to help solve real-life problems. Data on AIDS population by state is analyzed and the students actually map the trees in a park.

1. GIS is a real-life technological application that is being incorporated into the classroom. List two benefits of using this technology.

2. Suggest two other ways that GIS could be used in a high school classroom.

CHAPTER 7
PROJECT 1
ACCEPTABLE USE POLICY SEARCH

Visit the web sites of three school districts in your state and review their acceptable use policies. In a 1-2 page word-processed essay, compare the policies and describe how each policy would effect you and your students if you taught in that district. What precautions would you need to take to ensure that your students abide by the terms of the policies?

- Search the Web using a meta search engine such as Google (www.google.com) or Inference Find (www.inferencefind.com).
- Enter Acceptable Use Policy to get a sizable list of links to school systems.

CHAPTER 7
PROJECT 2
ON-LINE INTERACTION

Keeping in touch with the latest developments in education and particularly, educational technology, can be a challenging task. Participating in educational conferences and mailing lists (listservs) is one way to "keep in touch." Think of these services as a giant room of teachers talking with one another about all the things that teachers talk about.

Join one of the many conferences or listservs for educators you find on the Net. Follow the discussions for two weeks. In a 1-2 word-processed paper, identify the specific group you observed online. Summarize the type and usefulness of information received. How could you benefit from long-term participation in such an online group?

- Remember, all the communication is electronic, so you must have an email address to register.
- What happens at home when you don't check the U.S. mail regularly? The mail piles up! Check your mailbox frequently.
- You may want to participate as well as observe. You can respond or post a comment as well as read them. Be sure to identify yourself as a future teacher. Your future colleagues will most likely be helpful and supportive of you.

CHAPTER 7—FOR REFLECTION

1. Both synchronous and asynchronous communications are useful in education. List two of each form of communication and describe how you would use each one as a teacher. Which do you think is better, communicating at the same time or when communication is time-shifted?

2. Email programs often have many other features that are useful to organize oneself. Imagine that you are teaching in a school. Which three features of an email program would you use the most and why?

3. Internet Service Providers (ISPs) vary in the types of services they provide, the speed they connect, and with the quality of the connection. List the five most important attributes you would look for in an ISP and why.

CHAPTER 7 PUZZLER

www.CrosswordWeaver.com

Teaching and Learning with Technology

CHAPTER 7 PUZZLER CLUES

ACROSS

1 _____ markup language (HTML) is the language used to write web pages
3 _____ communications - occurs at the same time
5 _____ modem - a high-speed connection via the lines already installed for television
7 _____ reality provides a three-dimensional graphic environment that can be accessed on the Web
9 _____ interchange format - a file format used for color images, clip art, line art and gray-scale images
10 _____ communications - time-shifted
12 instant _____ is a one-to-one chat that can be started whenever another user is simultaneously online
14 an additional program needed to display multimedia in a web browser (use hyphen)
15 stands for Joint Photographic Expert Group, an agreed-upon standard for high-resolution images
17 Internet service _____ (ISPs) - special networks to provide home and business computers a way to connect to the Internet
18 a one-to-many communication where a message is posted for anyone to read, as if on a bulletin board
19 a search _____ is designed to find web sites based on key words
20 web _____ - a document that provides information and contains a series of hyperlinks to other resources
22 communication tool for networked environments (include hyphen)
23 _____ button - a graphic that is hyperlinked to another web page

DOWN

2 electronic communication between computers via telephone lines
4 _____ audio and video allows one to listen to audio or view a video clip as it is received by the browser
6 abbreviation for the method used for transferring files between computers on the Internet
8 web _____ - a collection of related web pages
11 a global network of networks connecting hundreds of millions of users
12 translates computer output into a format that is transmittable via telephone lines and then translates the signals back into a format that another computer can understand
13 a(n) _____ program is needed to open compressed files if they do not automatically expand after being downloaded
16 site that includes services such as a search engine, news, email, conferencing and chat rooms
18 _____ subscriber line (DSL) - a high-speed option to connect via phone lines
21 a site where two or more Internet users can meet in real time

CHAPTER 7 VIDEO REVIEW GUIDE

The following questions relate to the videos designated in the margins of chapter 7. Videos are available in My Lab School (www.mylabschool.com. Go to Courses/ Educational Technology/Video Lab or use the Assignment ID).

Video: *A Dinosaur WebQuest*
(Educational Technology, Methods to Classroom, Assignment ID ETV19)

Elementary school students are involved in a WebQuest, an inquiry-based activity that uses pre-researched web sites from the Internet. Students have specific tasks to complete. This WebQuest on dinosaurs covers areas in science and language arts.

1. List two things this teacher did to make it clear to students how to conduct their WebQuest.

2. Students in this video used a portal to conduct the WebQuest on dinosaurs. Explain what a portal is and describe how it is useful to teachers and students.

3. Discuss the problems students may encounter if a WebQuest is conducted without pre-selected web sites.

CHAPTER 8
PROJECT 1
WEB SITE EVALUATION

When using a web site for instruction, you must decide whether the information is of the quality you would like to use with your students. For this activity, choose any 3 web sites in the content area and/or grade level you would like to teach. Use the text web site evaluation rubric to determine their instructional quality. Select the one that scores the best. Then, in a 1-2 page paper describe how you could use this web site in your classroom. Give specific teaching and learning strategies that it would support.

- Look for web sites that support the intended instruction rather than web sites of sample lesson plans.
- If more than one web site scores equally on your rubrics, select the one you would most like to use for your lesson.

CHAPTER 8
PROJECT 2
CREATING NET-BASED LESSON PLANS

Research lesson plans at the grade level of your choice that use the Internet in a creative way. Select a lesson plan in each of the content areas below. The lesson plans might utilize key pals, a blog, a webcam or any number of Internet-based resources to help you teach or your students learn. Summarize the plans in a Best Internet Practices list to share with your peers. For each Best Practice choice, include

- Lesson Title
- Grade Level/Content Area
- URL
- A 2-3 sentence description of the lesson and how the Internet is used in it

Find lessons in each of these content areas:
- Math
- Science
- Social Studies
- Language Arts
- One other content area of your choice

CHAPTER 8—FOR REFLECTION

1. If you were to prepare a lesson on a subject matter that you are not very familiar with, how would you go about researching it with the resources available on the Internet today? How does that differ from the way research was conducted in the past, when there was no Internet?

2. Imagine that you are teaching in a school and you have the opportunity of creating a web site to support your classroom instruction. List five components that you want to include in this web site. How would you use each component and why did you select it?

3. When using the Internet with children, there are privacy and acceptable use issues. Describe the concerns and how you plan to address them when you become a teacher.

CHAPTER 8 PUZZLER

www.CrosswordWeaver.com

CHAPTER 8 PUZZLER CLUES

ACROSS

5 online _____ include current and archived articles of interest to educators

6 connection _____ are web sites that offer the opportunity to communicate with others with the same interests

7 these are interactive tools that not only include a pre-designed format, but ask customization questions in the process of creating a web page

9 web _____ tools assist a teacher in creating a web site

14 a function in browsers that assists one in collecting URLs by storing them

15 _____ tools include worksheet generators, such as puzzles, word searches, cryptograms, math exercises and multimedia flash cards

16 _____ reader is a free downloadable program to be able to read PDF files

17 abbreviation for frequently asked questions, a list of anticipated student questions that is posted on a classroom web site

18 pre-defined formats to make creating web pages or any word-processed document easier to lay out

19 teachers must be very conscious to guard this when including students' work or their images on a web site

20 also known as blogs, these are virtual online spaces for individuals to post personal commentary

21 action of limiting access to certain web sites that are not appropriate for students

22 abbreviation for the largest database of education information, with many of the documents and articles available through the Internet

23 _____ use policy articulates the ways in which the Internet can be used by students, and typically parents are asked to also sign this policy

DOWN

1 action of placing pages on a host site to have one's web site

2 _____ learning communities may be created by connecting a classroom with others across the globe, usually through student-to-student email

3 how easy or hard it is to move around a web site, how clear the links are, and whether a search engine is available on the site

4 test _____ create tests with randomly selected questions or pre-selected questions; they may be accessed online or can be converted into paper tests

8 classroom _____ tools are online resources, some of which are downloadable, that assist teachers in classroom tasks

10 the term that is usually typed on the subject line when one wants to discontinue receiving email from a mailing list

11 web _____ is a service offered by ISPs to make it possible for an individual to have his/her own web page or even a web site

12 electronic _____ lets you store and average students' grades

13 also known as bookmarks, it is a personal collection of URLs

17 program that is usually used to upload web pages onto a host site

Chapter 8—Using the Web for Teaching / Learning

Teaching and Learning with
Technology

CHAPTER 8 VIDEO REVIEW GUIDE

The following questions relate to the videos designated in the margins of chapter 8.
Videos are available in My Lab School (www.mylabschool.com. Go to Courses/
Educational Technology/Video Lab or use the Assignment ID).

Video: *Using Technology to Teach Reading*
(Educational Technology, Digital Text, Assignment ID ETV24)

Social studies teachers are helping seventh graders with low reading abilities with their
Internet research by using text readers (Kurzweil readers provide audio of the text on
the screen). This assistance with reading is giving the students confidence and
allowing them to concentrate on their social studies lesson.

1. Describe the logistics with the use of computers in this class – how many
   computers, how many students on each computer, etc.

2. What kind of preparation do the teachers have to make to ensure that students are
   finding web sites that are authoritative and credible? How do they assist the
   students in organizing their note-taking?

3. How do these teachers bring aspects of other subjects into this social studies
   lesson?

Video: *The GLOBE Project*
(Educational Technology, GLOBE, Assignment ID ETV15)

GLOBE — Global Learning and Observation to Benefit the Environment — is a worldwide science project where students collect local data and then input the information onto the GLOBE web site. This allows students at other sites to compare their data with others.

1. List the different technologies used in the GLOBE Project.

2. How does the GLOBE Project connect students to their world?

3. How else could students connect to other students? What are the benefits of connecting students around the world?

Video: *Using a Class Web Page for Learning*
(Educational Technology, Mentorships, Assignment ID ETV9)

This French language teacher uses a class web page and email to provide students with resources for their online WebQuest assignment.

1. This French teacher has a web page where she has placed resources for a biography project. List several of the resources she has on her web page.

2. What other resources could this teacher have added to her web page that would be useful to students?

Video: *Wireless WebQuest*
(Educational Technology, A University and Rural School Division Partnership, Assignment ID ETV7)

A student teacher uses a WebQuest to teach students about Edgar Allan Poe and his writings. Students are using wireless laptops.

1. Describe how this teacher set up his lesson on Edgar Allan Poe – the classroom setting and the resources used?

2. In addition to learning about Edgar Allan Poe and his writings, what other skills are these students gaining?

3. This teacher indicated that he found the WebQuest he selected on the Web. How would you go about searching the Internet for resources on lesson plans such as WebQuests?

CHAPTER 9
PROJECT 1
TEACHER OBSERVATION

The purpose of this project is to help you to become aware of how audiovisual technologies are used for instruction. Observe an instructor who uses traditional and/or digital audiovisual technologies in their classroom. In a 1-2 page word-processed report, briefly describe the instructional setting; what technologies were used; how they were used; the teacher and student skills that were necessary to use the technologies; and the student responses to the lesson as well as why the technologies were or were not as effective as you expected. You may want to review and use the rubrics in the text to help you assess the effectiveness of the media you observe.

CHAPTER 9
PROJECT 2
CREATE AN INSTRUCTIONAL VIDEO

Prepare a lesson plan using the DID model that can best be supported by a brief video. You will be making the video you describe in your lesson. For the video you will first story board it, then create it, and finally critique it. The steps are detailed below.

- **Storyboarding** - Before preparing any lengthy presentation utilizing a series of visuals, it is important to organize the presentation well in advance. Storyboarding is an effective technique for doing this. Create a 10 card storyboard for a videotape you will each be creating for this course. Each card should include the image to be used in each shot, some detail on the narrative to go with the shot, and production instructions, such as when to zoom in or do close-ups. Review Interchapter 9 for storyboarding instructions.
- **Creating the Video** - Using the video plan detailed in your storyboards, create a 5-10 minute teaching video that presents the topic of your lesson plan to the grade level of your choice.
- **Critiquing your Video** - After you have completed taping, in a 1-2 page word-processed document, critique your own video. Be sure to comment on the following
  - How could I improve upon my verbal delivery?
  - How could I improve upon the visual image I presented?
  - Were my props effective? What could I have done better?

CHAPTER 9—FOR REFLECTION

1. Give one or two examples of audio technologies that were used when you were in middle school (perhaps a record player). How have those technologies been transformed and what has replaced them today?

2. Give two examples of visual technologies that were used when you were in middle school (it could even be as simple as the chalkboard). How have those technologies been transformed and what has replaced them today?

3. Multimedia encompasses multiple media combined into a single integrated whole. Considering that there are three basic learning styles: auditory, visual and kinesthetic, what do you think are the advantages of using multimedia in a classroom presentation or in a piece of software, rather than strictly audio or visual technologies?

CHAPTER 9 PUZZLER

CHAPTER 9 PUZZLER CLUES

ACROSS

4 _____ files—a common format for digital Internet audio
6 consists of several elements presented in a deliberate arrangement
10 _____ camera - uses a video camera mounted on a stand that captures and projects images placed below it
11 _____ transmission - signals are sent up into space and then sent back down elsewhere on Earth
13 _____ TV (CCTV) is a network of television monitors connected via coaxial cables throughout a school building (includes a hyphen)
16 abbreviation for the disc used to store both video and audio, allows for hours of playback
18 _____ material - visual displays such as books, worksheets, posters and charts
20 able to hear and comprehend
21 land-based
22 includes drawings, cartoons and diagrams that represent and clarify concepts and relationships
23 _____ board - a flexible surface that can be changed easily
24 the act of sending signals up to a satellite
26 used in classrooms to write and display - they are now being replaced by whiteboards
28 _____ chart allows for written text that can be saved on a pad or torn off and displayed
31 _____ listening - giving your full attention to the auditory stimulus
32 economical, durable, easy-to-use magnetic medium that allows the recording of voice, music or other sounds
33 _____ technologies are needed because digitized video files are very large and take a very long time to transmit across the Internet
34 thin sheets of clear acetate that may be used to write or print, used on an overhead projector

DOWN

1 _____ audio is received through a radio
2 oral _____ - usually an interview captured on an audiotape related to a single event
3 may include a diorama or classroom display
5 _____ recorders (VCRs)
6 broadcast _____ - commonly known as television
7 _____ projector - displays transparent visuals by shining a powerful lamp from below
8 a compact video camera recorder used to record sound and images, may be played back through a VCR
9 _____ book - adds an auditory dimension to a text
12 _____ television - uses broadcast airwaves to distribute video signals throughout a school district
14 _____ video technology compresses and plays back digital video while it is being received
15 _____ disc, or CD, stores digital audio
17 _____ projectors are computer outputs that can project images
19 provides a slick surface to be used with special colored markers
25 abbreviation for a terrestrial system that sends signals via microwave transmission from a studio to specific broadcast locations
27 visual _____ allows an individual to accurately interpret visuals
29 _____ audio - downloadable digital audio
30 a three-dimensional representation of concepts or real objects

CHAPTER 9 VIDEO REVIEW GUIDE

The following questions relate to the videos designated in the margins of chapter 9. Videos are available in My Lab School (www.mylabschool.com. Go to Courses/ Educational Technology/Video Lab or use the Assignment ID).

Video: *Using Visuals in Learning*
(Educational Technology, Assessment in Action, Assignment ID ETV11)

This video demonstrates the use of visuals in the classroom via a lesson on China. It also examines the usefulness of videotaping a student teacher's lesson for assessment and feedback.

1. List several of the visuals that are shown in this video.

2. What other audiovisual technologies could the teacher have chosen to teach the unit on China?

3. This video also discusses the advantages of videotaping a student teacher. Give two reasons why it is a useful process.

CHAPTER 10
PROJECT 1
DISTANCE EDUCATION IN K-12 STATE COMPARISON

Many states and districts have instituted opportunities for students in public schools to use distance delivered courses. Use the Internet to research the opportunities in your state. Compare your findings to at least one other state that offers abundant distance education opportunities to public school students. Create a table that compares your state to the other state you research on the following key criteria:
- Classes offered
- Media used for delivery
- Location of meetings if any
- Location of and access to teacher
- How are the following handled:
  - Presentation and lectures
  - Homework collection and grading
  - Tests
  - Student-to-teacher interaction
  - Student-to-student interaction
  - Limitations on who can take the courses
  - Costs or other charges
  - Any other noteworthy criteria you wish to add
- Conclude with your view of the pros, cons, and usefulness of your state's K-12 distance education program.

CHAPTER 10
PROJECT 2
ISSUES IN ONLINE LEARNING

There are many issues, both academic and working condition, that are associated with teaching a distance education class. Much discussion is currently underway on these issues, much of it posted on teacher organization web sites. Review the issues related to teaching at a distance and, based on your research, respond to the following questions. Add any other issues you discover in your research as well. Be sure to support your responses with information from your research.
- Is distance delivered instruction of the same quality as traditional instruction?
- How does teaching a distance education class impact a teacher's workload?
- How can behavior and cheating be managed in a distance environment?
- What kinds of technology need to be acquired for distance delivery? Is the investment in distance education technology worth the return?
- How do the advantages and costs of offering distance classes compare?

CHAPTER 10—FOR REFLECTION

1. Have you had any distance education experiences? Try to remember the benefits and the disadvantages of that experience. If you have not had a distance education experience, try to imagine what it would be like and what characteristics of it you would like and dislike. Why?

2. Reflecting on your experiences with language arts, mathematics, history, science, music, which ones do you think would be adaptable for distance education and which ones would not? Why? Would there be a difference in adaptability depending on grade level?

3. Select the five distance learning technologies that you would prefer to use if you were teaching a distance education course. Reflect on your teaching style and your students' learning styles and how each of the selected technologies would be received, depending on the students' learning styles.

CHAPTER 10 PUZZLER

www.CrosswordWeaver.com

CHAPTER 10 PUZZLER CLUES

ACROSS

1 _____ classroom - another term for distance education
3 _____ instruction - useful in distance education, provides content divided into manageable units of material
6 required of teachers and students to work within a new environment - distance education
8 _____ call - an audio option for communication where several participants (usually 3 to 8) can connect together
12 instantaneous delivery of graphics or text via a telephone line
16 or assessment, a key issue in distance education since traditional testing is not available
17 the most basic of telephone conference system
20 _____ mail - allows for written messages to be sent through the Internet, provides for attachments such as graphics, audio and compressed video files
21 _____ site - may be used to combine synchronous and asynchronous resources so that students in a class may have a single virtual space
22 often used to determine whether a student's learning style and study habits are such that they may be successful in a distance education format
23 _____ mail - allows for audio messages to be left via a telephone
25 _____ education - delivery of instruction to students who are separated from their teacher by time and/or location

DOWN

2 supports - readily available in a traditional classroom, must be planned for in distance education, may include telephone or online homework assistance
4 _____ learning - another term for distance education
5 time-shifted
7 at the same time
9 allows the creation of interactive classrooms across a school district or state
10 _____ courses - earliest distance-delivery system
11 _____ system - used in distance education as a contingency plan for anticipated problems
13 must be planned in distance education for it to occur between student and teacher and among students
14 must be planned in distance education because body language and other ways for students to communicate are not available
15 phone _____ allows up to 50 callers to connect together via the telephone
18 electronic _____ - offers a platform for one-to-many communication, also called an electronic forum
19 _____ support - critical when implementing distance learning systems
24 Internet _____ allows for many users to communicate within the same virtual space

CHAPTER 10 VIDEO REVIEW GUIDE

The following questions relate to the videos designated in the margins of chapter 6. Videos are available in My Lab School (www.mylabschool.com. Go to Courses/ Educational Technology/Video Lab or use the Assignment ID).

Video: *Virtual School*
(Educational Technology, Florida Virtual School Part I, Assignment ID ETV32)

The Florida Virtual School provides distance education for students as a statewide choice for K-12 public education. This segment describes its founding as well as how the curriculum was developed.

1. This video explains that the Florida Virtual School had only a 50% success rate the first year it was in operation. How was this low success rate improved in the following years?

2. Describe how the curriculum was developed and how it was evaluated.

3. Summarize the steps that you should take if you were asked to develop a distance education course.

Video: *Options for Virtual Students*
(Educational Technology, Florida Virtual School Part II, Assignment ID ETV33)

This video shows how different students benefit from enrolling in the Florida Virtual School. Students may enroll full-time and complete all their courses through the Virtual School. Other students may enroll in one or two courses to supplement their regular school offerings.

1. List several reasons, as reported by the students in this video, why they like the Florida Virtual School.

2. What are other advantages to students if states offer courses online?

CHAPTER 11
PROJECT 1
FAIR USE GUIDELINES WORKSHOP

Complete an Internet search of the guidelines that must be observed to legally use multimedia components in your classroom. After searching at least TWO sources, prepare a PowerPoint presentation that you might share in a workshop on Fair Use. Include how each of the components below can be utilized in your classroom without violating copyright laws.

- Digital media from the Internet
- Text
- Artwork
- Music, speech or sound clips
- Videos or video clips
- Photographs

Be sure to include the sources of your information at the bottom of the document. Your sources should be authorities in the field (e.g. organizations, law offices, court decisions, educational institutions) rather than an individual's opinions.

CHAPTER 11
PROJECT 2
CLASSROOM OF TOMORROW

Use the Internet to search and review futurist articles on how classrooms and instruction is likely to change with the advent of emerging technologies. Create a diagram of the classroom of tomorrow with a supporting word-processed document describing 1) the technologies you envision being there, 2) how instruction will be altered as a result of those technologies and 3) how your role and activities as a teacher might change when teaching in this classroom.

After reading through future-looking research and web sites such as Microsoft, Thornburg's web site, Apple, etc., let you imagination go and try to anticipate your teaching future with technology.

CHAPTER 11—FOR REFLECTION

1. Assume that you are a parent of a fifth-grade student. Your child tells you that the class has developed a class web site and that every student's name and address will be available on the web site as a classroom directory. Also, every student can select his or her own favorite web site to link to the class web page. What concerns do you have as a parent and how would you approach the school to address these concerns?

2. Imagine that you are a high school social sciences teacher. You have assigned students a ten-page research paper. How do you set-up the assignment to make it clear that plagiarism will not be tolerated and what tools would you use to check for plagiarism? What steps would you take if a student's paper is found to have been copied in parts from the Internet?

3. Imagine the perfect classroom of the future. Describe what technologies you would have available for students. Which ones would you have them use individually, which ones in small groups, and which technologies could be used by the classroom as a whole? If possible, try to imagine new technologies that are not available yet.

Chapter 11—Implementing Technology in Schools

CHAPTER 11 PUZZLER

CHAPTER 11 PUZZLER CLUES

ACROSS

1 _____ intelligence - software programs that function the way the human brain works

5 _____ software - compares a student's written work with authors' work as well as work posted on the Web

9 _____ planning - a long-range plan that follows a series of defined steps

10 _____ environment - immersion allowed by technology to be able to feel, smell, taste, see, and hear aspects of the environment

12 _____ networking - connects computers to a server without the need for cables

13 _____ systems - artificial intelligence programs that offer suggestions and advice on the basis of a database of expertise

17 _____ literacy - in this Digital Age, as basic a skill as reading

19 code of _____ for computer use is a set of written expectations and definitions of what is acceptable use

20 _____ network - software that is able to learn and adjust its responses on the basis of previous interactions

21 academic _____ - problems occurring due to the ease of manipulating and sharing of digital data

23 a right that every citizen has, creates significant issues in the Digital Age, both in society and in education

24 _____-___-_____networking - a communication alternative where computers are connected together directly

DOWN

1 intelligent _____ - artificial intelligence programs that help with specific tasks by asking questions, monitor work and perform requested tasks

2 blending of technologies into a single multipurpose technology

3 _____ divide - inequity of access to technology

4 a common wireless networking technology, based on the common 802.11 standard

6 comes from the Hawaiian term for fast - it is a web site in which content is written collaboratively so that anyone who can access the site may edit and add information

7 _____ software - does not allow connection to unacceptable Internet sites

8 a discounted cost for telecommunications service for schools, libraries and other similar community entities (include a hyphen)

11 _____ use - issues surrounding the use of technology so that it protects students from inappropriate behaviors and information

14 as related to software, sharing with others or installing on multiple machines when only one copy has been purchased

15 laws that protect the interests of those who own creative works

16 freedom of _____ - a significant issue of ethical concern, whereby content on the Internet is not regulated because of this and therefore students may find objectionable and inappropriate material online

18 _____ logic software - artificial intelligence programs that resemble human decision making

22 _____ use - describe circumstances under which a teacher can use copyrighted materials in face-to-face instruction

CHAPTER 11 VIDEO REVIEW GUIDE

The following questions relate to the videos designated in the margins of chapter 11. Videos are available in My Lab School (www.mylabschool.com. Go to Courses/ Educational Technology/Video Lab or use the Assignment ID).

Video: *Universal Design for Special Needs*
(Educational Technology, Assistive Technologies and Universal Design, Assignment ID ETV13)

The principle of universal design requires that products should be designed to meet the needs of all individuals. This video discusses how universal design comes about, through a process that starts with advocacy, then accommodation and eventually accessibility. Technologies that make learning accessible to all students should be infused through the curriculum.

1. According to this video, accessibility does not happen overnight. Describe the steps in the development of accessibility.

2. Give two examples of universal design available in computers today.

3. Identify two different types of disabilities that teachers may encounter among their students.

4. Describe how a universal design textbook might work for a student with cognitive disabilities.

CHAPTER 12
PROJECT 1
STANDARDS AND ACCOMPLISHED PRACTICES

Search the Internet to review the Educator Accomplished Practices identified as essential for your state. If no formal statement of Accomplished Practices has been articulated in your state, instead review the National Board standards for teachers to identify the practices an excellent teacher should demonstrate.

The National Board standards can be found at www.nbpts.org. After your review, in a one to two page word-processed essay, explain how technology is or can be incorporated into these critical standards for teaching excellence. Justify your reasons for technology integration. What will you do to ensure you achieve the technology competency the practices and standards call for? Be sure to identify your sources and use APA style for your citations.

CHAPTER 12
PROJECT 2
BUILDING YOUR TECHNOLOGY SKILLS

Complete the technology competency checklist in Interchapter 12. In a self-reflective essay, describe your current overall level of technology skills. Do you feel your skills are adequate? If yes, explain why and how you will continue to maintain your current skill level. If not, what can you do to achieve the level you need when you teach?

Research courses at your local college and in-service programs at your local district and create an annotated list of workshops and/or courses you feel you should take to achieve or maintain the technology competency you desire.

CHAPTER 12—FOR REFLECTION

1. Consider your level of educational technology literacy as you complete this course. How competent do you believe you are in order to teach in a technology-rich environment? What other opportunities would you search for to become even more proficient in the use of technology in the classroom?

2. Project 10 years into the future. You have now been a classroom teacher for the past 7-8 years. Technology has probably changed significantly between the time you completed your student teaching and now. What options have you considered – and perhaps taken – to stay current in technology?

3. Once again, consider that it is 10 years in the future and that you have been teaching for 7-8 years. What kind of support would you expect, or wish for, from the school's media specialist as well as the school principal and assistant principals?

CHAPTER 12 PUZZLER

www.CrosswordWeaver.com

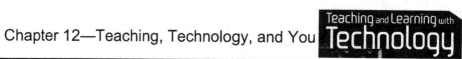

CHAPTER 12 PUZZLER CLUES

ACROSS

1 abbreviation for the ISTE standards for teachers (includes one hyphen)
5 technology _____ provide teachers and administrators with direction and guidance for creating programs that incorporate technology while meeting the needs of students
8 teacher _____ or certification is required in all states for individuals to be employed as educators
12 abbreviation for the foundational document that established ISTE's NETS-A standards
13 abbreviation for a national educational technology organization that has developed technology standards for teachers and students
14 _____ requirements are set by each state's Department of Education for employment as educators
15 _____ specialists - new term for school librarians, recognizes their expanded role
16 abbreviation for a federal law which includes technology education standards
17 _____ learning is required of many professions, including teachers
18 _____ practices - requirements dictate the expectations for educational professionals

DOWN

1 abbreviation for the ISTE standards for administrators
2 abbreviation for a nonprofit, nongovernmental agency focused on improving teaching and learning by encouraging teachers to become nationally certified
3 abbreviation for the ISTE standards for students
4 _____ development - ongoing education and training required of all educators
6 abbreviation for the national accrediting agency for teacher education programs
7 _____ teachers - those individuals in teacher education programs preparing to become teachers
8 educational technology _____ for teachers includes not only how being able to use technology but to know how to apply the technologies to enrich their teaching and their students' learning
9 _____ certification - available, in addition to state licensure, recognizes teachers for having met professional teaching standards
10 certification _____ - most states require ongoing professional development for their educators to maintain their certificate or license, usually every three to five years
11 __-_____ teachers - individuals who are currently serving as educators

CHAPTER 12 VIDEO REVIEW GUIDE

The following questions relate to the videos designated in the margins of chapter 12. Videos are available in My Lab School (www.mylabschool.com. Go to Courses/ Educational Technology/Video Lab or use the Assignment ID).

Video: *State Technology Planning*
(Educational Technology, Overview of a Statewide System, Assignment ID ETV14)

The State of Louisiana has developed a statewide technology plan that involves K-12 school districts as well as Colleges of Education. This statewide plan started as a small grant in five pilot sites and has grown to include the integration of technology across the state. It included funding to build the infrastructure as well as professional development for teachers.

1. Describe the incremental steps that the state of Louisiana took as it developed a statewide technology plan.

2. What other steps were taken at the state level to maintain the momentum of the initial project?

3. List different approaches that states can take to promote technology use in the classroom.

Video: *QUEST Training for Teachers*
(Educational Technology, Overview of a Statewide System, Assignment ID ETV14)

Louisiana used a PT3 grant to develop a statewide professional development program which they named T.H.E. QUEST (Technology and Higher Education Quality Education for Students and Teachers). It includes training teachers and university faculty in how to incorporate technology into their curriculum.

1. Why is it necessary to provide training to university faculty in teacher education programs?

2. At how many levels does this statewide technology training affect the use of technology in the state of Louisiana?

3. List other resources, besides statewide projects, that current teachers can utilize to enhance their technology training.

Video: *Staff Development for Online Learning*
(Educational Technology, Florida Virtual School Part I, Assignment ID ETV32)

The Florida Virtual School has developed a process to prepare teachers for online teaching. Before teaching in the Virtual School, teachers must enroll in three online courses. Support from mentors and telephone conferences during the first year of teaching in an online environment are critical to the success of the Virtual School.

1. The video discusses some of the characteristics that set the Florida Virtual School apart from other schools. List two differences.

2. Describe the steps taken to prepare teachers for teaching online in the Florida Virtual School.

3. How are teachers supported once they start teaching in the online environment of the Florida Virtual School?

COURSE
ACTIVITIES

PROBLEM-BASED LEARNING SCENARIOS

SCENARIO 1
WHAT WOULD YOU DO?

Scenario

Your district has invested funds in a new program to refocus instruction so that it meets the unique needs of learners. It is encouraging every teacher to become familiar with the learning styles, cognitive styles, and multiple intelligences of the students in their classroom.

To that end the district has provided you with age-appropriate instruments that will supply you with the information needed to develop a profile of your students. It has also created and offered a series of training workshops to help you interpret the results. With these tools and the district's support, you will be able to know your students precisely enough to create a learning environment and target instruction to meet their individual and collective needs.

Within the framework of this program, the district has offered to fund purchase requests that will help each teacher to create a classroom learning environment that supports the aspects of student diversity that are identified through these instruments. You and your colleagues see an opportunity to better meet the needs of your students while renewing and improving your classrooms through this initiative.

Currently your typical classroom has:
- 28 student desks
- A teachers desk with chair
- Two computers for student use on a table with two chairs
- A monitor and VCR on a cart
- Two student tables with four chairs
- One book case
- One four-drawer filing cabinet
- One full-size white board
- One full-size bulletin board

Problem

You and your colleagues are anxious to use this district initiative to acquire new furniture, equipment, and educational technologies for your classroom. You attend a workshop to find out the process to improve your classroom. At the workshop, your principal has asked that each department and/or grade level interested in applying work together to develop an ideal learning environment that will support individualized instruction to meet diverse learner needs. The ideal learning environment descriptions must include everything a teacher wants from furniture to miscellaneous equipment to technologies.

The principal has specifically stated that to submit a request for funds from the district, each team must:
- Diagram their idea of an ideal classroom learning environment
- Identify and justify all acquisitions
- Develop an instructional design on the topic of your choice that demonstrates full utilization of your ideal classroom

You and your colleagues have been managing without many of the technologies, furniture, and resources that you would like to have had for the past two years. You are determined to use this opportunity to turn each of your classrooms into an ideal learning environment you have always wanted for your students.

What Would You Do?

Towards A Solution

You and your colleagues need to work together to meet the requirements set forth by your principal. The steps you may wish to follow might include:
- Researching the technologies, furniture, equipment, and other resources that help to address learning styles, cognitive styles, and/or multiple intelligences.
- Meeting with your colleagues to verbally brainstorm what the ideal learning environment would include.
- Creating a formal list or a mind map of all the technology, furniture, equipment, or other resources you want to buy.
- Creating a classroom floor plan of your ideal learning environment in which you arrange and place all of your target acquisitions
- Deciding upon a topic and developing an instructional design using the DID model that utilizes your new acquisitions.
- Presenting your diagram, list of acquisitions with justifications, and your instructional design in a professional package for presentation to your principal.

Problem-Based Learning Activity

In a group of up to four, work with your peers to solve the problem presented in this scenario. You may use the steps articulated in the *Towards a Solution* section or you can customize it to your group's needs or you may decide on an entirely different approach to solving the problem presented in the scenario.

Your goal is to complete the task details so that you have a product you can submit to make your classroom an ideal environment for teaching and learning. Work through all aspects of the scenario until you have created what your hypothetical principal has requested. Be prepared to turn in your final product and to present your solution to your peers.

PROBLEM-BASED LEARNING SCENARIOS

SCENARIO 2
WHAT WOULD YOU DO?

Scenario

At the urging of your school and district, your grade level (or department) has decided to enter the Information Age and create a web site. The school has provided easy-to-use web authoring tools and has offered to link your web site to the school home page. You and your fellow teachers are reasonably computer literate and should have little problem actually creating your pages. You also have additional help from the tech support department at your school. You have decided to meet together to discuss how to plan for and organize the web site. The only guidelines you have are the district general guidelines for school web sites. The pertinent district guidelines you need to be aware of are as follows:

- Web sites must include the school name and contact information.
- Web sites should introduce the teacher(s) who created the site.
- All web sites should have some academic purpose.
- To protect the safety of the students, web sites should not include individual student pictures or names.
- Web sites should provide information to and support the participation of the community.
- Web sites should provide useful information to students and their parents.

Beyond these guidelines, you and your colleagues are free to organize and create a grade level (or departmental) web site of your own choosing. You may want to have a consistent theme on the home page that is carried through to each individual classroom page. You may want to join your own unique and diverse pages together and connect them to a single home page. You may want to have common elements that appear on all classroom pages or you may prefer to have every page entirely unique. How you design your web site and your individual classroom page is your choice as long as the site conforms to district guidelines.

Problem

You and your colleagues, while computer literate, have never thought about how to join your grade level (or department) together for presentation on the Web. Some of your colleagues are very organized and will no doubt want a very simple, no-nonsense web site. Others are highly creative and will want to create an innovative site that stands out on the school and district site.

You have all agreed that you want your web site to help your students academically. It should

also help them and parents stay involved in the activities of your school and your classroom. You want to be able to post notices to parents about upcoming events, current homework, and important dates. You want to offer students who are absent from class a way to keep up with what they have missed. You want to highlight every student's achievement in some way. You also want to make it possible for parents to interact with you via the Web through email. You have decided to make your grade level or department web site as meaningful and useful as it is attractive to view and interact with. Your meeting with your peers is this week. You need to bring some ideas to the table so that this project can get underway. Your principal has asked that those creating web sites have them read to go live in two months.

What Would You Do?

Towards A Solution

Before attending the first meeting, you may want to explore web sites from other schools that include links to grade level or departmental sites similar to the one your are planning. When exploring those sites:

- Use your web site evaluation rubric to determine what you like best about the site
- Note any special web site features you feel are especially useful
- Examine the web sites you review in light of your district's guidelines and note how those sites conform

You and your colleagues then need to meet to develop your plan for your web site. The steps you may wish to follow might include:
- Meeting with your colleagues to verbally brainstorm what the web site home page should include and what each classroom page should include.
- Decide on any common appearance or theme for your site
- Creating a diagram or mind map showing how all pages of the site are linked.
- Identify the features to be included on the grade level or departmental home page as well as the features that classroom pages should include.
- Articulate how your site meets each of the district standards.
- Prepare to orally and visually present the plan for your site to your principal.

Problem-Based Learning Activity

With up to four of your peers, prepare a hypothetical grade level or departmental web site that includes your own classroom sites that meets all of the district guidelines. You may use the steps articulated in the *Towards a Solution* section or you may decide on an entirely different approach to solving the problem presented in the scenario. Your goal is to fully articulate and diagram your hypothetical grade level web site including the classroom web sites for each of your peers. Work through all aspects of the scenario until you have created and can diagram

PROBLEM-BASED LEARNING SCENARIOS

SCENARIO 3
WHAT WOULD YOU DO?

Scenario

For the current academic year, you have served on your school's Technology Committee. As a result you have learned about the many technologies that can help you and your colleagues teach and your students learn. You have become excited by the possibilities and have changed the way you teach to incorporate more technologies. Your have found your lessons are more exciting as a result and your students are more engaged. You have noticed that most of your colleagues don't seem to share your enthusiasm for technology. While you are somewhat concerned about this, you are not surprised since they did not have the same opportunities that you have had to become familiar with educational technology while serving on the technology committee. You are fairly certain that if they had, your colleagues too would embrace technology and use its potential.

Your principal has asked the Technology Committee to formulate a strategic plan for technology for next year. The plan will include all aspects of acquiring and implementing technology in your school. The committee has decided to manage the work by breaking it into tasks to be addressed by subcommittees. You have been asked to chair the subcommittee that will develop the portion of the strategic plan that will address how best to integrate technology into curriculum and into every teacher's instruction. Your job will be to develop ideas for motivating and inspiring your colleagues as well as to develop suggestions for improving access to technology for your fellow teachers.

Problem

You and your colleagues share a belief in technology's potential in the classroom. However, you are concerned about the best way to orient your peers to that potential, train them in various technologies, and encourage them to fully integrate technology into instruction.

After discussions with your principal and voicing your concerns about how best to encourage and motivate the other teachers in your school, your principal has offered to set aside $5,000 of the school budget for mini-grants to encourage your peers in technology integration. She has also asked the school Technology Coordinator to work with you to develop and deliver technology training sessions as needed.

You and your colleagues need to develop a year-long plan, backed by your principal's support and funding, to help your fellow teachers embrace and use the technological resources at their disposal.

What Would You Do?

Towards A Solution

To approach this problem, it may be best to begin with the standards by which teacher and student technology competencies are measured. These standard articulate the professional expectations for teachers in terms of technology. These are very often adopted by states and districts and are typically used for benchmarks in strategic plans. ISTE's NETS Standards for teachers and students (http://cnets.iste.org) are the definitive standards but other organizations also provide guidelines that are useful measures for determining necessary technology competencies. You may also wish to check the technology standards provided by the National Council for Accreditation of Teacher Education (NCATE at http://www.ncate.org/ standard/m_stds.htm); International Technology Education Association (ITEA at http:// www.iteawww.org); Southeast Regional Education Board (SERB at http://www.sreb.org); North Central Regional Technology Education Consortium (NCRTEC at http://www.ncrtec.org/pd/ tssa/tssa.pdf); and National Commission on Teaching and America's Future (NCATF at http:// www/nctaf.org).

You may also wish to explore school strategic plans available on the Web to see how other schools are addressing teacher preparation and technology integration. Further, you may wish to examine training and grant programs at various districts to see how these techniques are working to encourage teachers to use technology.

You and your colleagues will need to meet to brainstorm what your fellow teachers need to know and what is needed to encourage them to fully embrace and integrate technology. Then, you will need to develop a plan that includes initiatives that accomplish this goal.

Problem-Based Learning Activity

With up to four of your peers, review national and/or local standards and decide upon those that you feel should be met by your group's strategic planning efforts. Once the scope of work as defined by standards is determined, prepare a plan for teacher training and technology integration that articulates:

- Ideas for motivating teachers to embrace and use technology
- Methods for awarding the mini-grants authorized by your principal
- A training program that should be available to faculty
- Technologies that should be made available to faculty as professional resources
- Technologies that should be made available to faculty for their classrooms

You may use a plan format that is based on the suggestions in your text or that is similar to a plan you have found on the Internet. It should, however, include goals and strategies that will achieve your technology integration goals. Be prepared to turn in your plan and to present your solution to your class.

IN THE FIELD ACTIVITIES

The following activities offer structured experiences that help you to observe and investigate educational technology in action. These experiences assist you in examining how educational technology is reviewed, selected and implemented in the classroom and in schools from both an academic and administrative perspective. Through these experiences, you will be able to expand your understanding and enhance your ability to make judgments regarding the skills, methods, and educational technologies best used to enhance teaching and learning.

Goal

The purpose of the educational technology observation experience is for the student to see how a educational technology is reviewed, selected and implemented in the classroom and in schools. As a result the student will be able to make value judgments regarding the skills and educational technologies that can be used to enhance teaching and learning.

Objectives

The student will be able to:
- Identify instructional applications of educational technologies in the classroom and throughout the school
- Contrast the roles of the various school professionals in selecting and implementing educational technologies
- Evaluate the effectiveness of key technologies observed in action

Areas to Observe

- Physical appearance of the classroom including the arrangement of all components
- Educational technologies and related materials available
- Learning activities that involve technology
- Teaching strategies using educational technologies
- Assessment strategies using educational technologies
- Student involvement and attitudes relating to educational technologies
- Curriculum utilizing support technologies
- School organization

In The Field Activity 1
Technology in the Learning Space

1. Describe the technologies available to the teacher and to the learners in this classroom.

2. After observing the classroom in action, explain how the arrangement and technologies in this space help student learning.

3. In what ways, if any, do they hinder student learning?

4. In what ways does this learning space meet the needs of diverse learners?

5. What technologies seem particularly effective in meeting learner needs? Give examples.

6. What technologies should be added to this learning space to make it more effective? How does the teacher compensate for these lacking technologies?

7. What would you change in this learning space to make it more effective for you as the teacher and for your students?

On the next sheet, draw a diagram showing the placement of teacher, students, and furnishings. Note how the technologies in this classroom are arranged.

86

DIAGRAM THE CLASSROOM

IN THE FIELD ACTIVITY 2
TEACHER INTERVIEW ON TECHNOLOGY

Interview a teacher at the grade level or content area you would like to teach. Ask the teacher the following questions. Feel free to elaborate or ask additional questions in response to the answers you are given.

- What is your name and position? How long have you been teaching?

- Which three technologies do you use most often when you teach? Why do you like to use those best?

- Which classroom technologies do you most often assign to your students to help them learn? What types of activities are completed using each of these technologies?

- When you plan your lessons, how do you decide which methods and technologies to use?

- How did you select the types of technologies in your classroom?

- If you want to add additional technologies to you classroom, how do you go about it?

- Is there a committee at your school that addresses a teacher's needs for technology in the classroom? If so, who serves on it and how do you communicate your needs to that committee?

- What would you say is the most important thing a new teacher should know or do to use technology effectively in teaching and learning?

IN THE FIELD ACTIVITY 3
UNDERSTANDING THE ROLE OF THE MEDIA CENTER

Visit a school Media Center and talk to the media specialist to help you answer the following questions.

- What kinds of media and equipment are available for teachers and students to use in the Media Center? What is available to check out?

- What is the process a teacher needs to follow in order to use or checkout media from the Media Center?

- If a teacher would like resources to be made available in the Media Center, how does he or she go about requesting they be ordered?

- What kind of budget does the Media Center typically have to purchase new equipment or resources? Who makes the decision as to what to buy?

- With reference to computers in the Media Center for student use:

  -What is the ratio of computers to number of students using the Media Center?

  -Are these computers networked or stand-alone? Are printers available?

  -What software is available on them and do they have Internet access?

  -What is done to ensure students are conforming to the school's acceptable use policies?

  -Are community members able to use these computers during after school hours or for special activities?

- How do the technologies and resources available in the Media Center complement those found in the classroom?

IN THE FIELD ACTIVITY 4
TECHNOLOGY FROM THE ADMINISTRATIVE VIEWPOINT

For this activity you may want to talk to an administrator and a technology support specialist to fully answer each question.

- Does this school and the district have a technology plan? Who creates them and how are they related to each other?

- How are decisions made as to which technologies should be purchased and where they should be placed in the school?

- If a teacher would like a technology for his or her classroom, what is the process that must be followed to get it?

- If a problem arises with a technology in the classroom, who does the teacher turn to for help and support? How long does it usually take to get a problem resolved?

- What kinds of training are available for teachers to learn how to use hardware and software?

- Is there a technology committee active in the school? What input does it have on technology decision making?

- Are there any events or activities that involve the community with the school's technology?

- What are this school's best features related to technology in teaching and learning? What are its greatest problems?

IN THE FIELD ACTIVITY 5
ISSUES IN IMPLEMENTING TECHNOLOGY

For this activity you may want to talk to an administrator and/or technology support specialist as well as to a teacher to prepare to answer each question.

1. How does this school protect its network and the privacy of the students?

2. What is the acceptable use policy? How is it explained to students?

3. How are students protected from visiting inappropriate sites on the Internet?

4. What parental permissions must be granted for students to use the school's technology? What is the process for getting this permission?

5. How does this school handle connecting and supporting diverse kinds of computer hardware and software? What happens when a computer gets too old to use?

6. What emerging technologies are being considered for this school or for other schools in the district?

7. What district-wide software is used for administrative functions such as attendance or grades?

8. Does this school distribute computers to individual classrooms, in computer labs, or both? If there are labs, how are they used?

9. What are the stated policies of the school with regard to piracy? What steps are taken to ensure students do not pirate software?

10. Do you feel that this school has done an effective job in addressing the key issues related to using technology in schools? Why or why not?

IN THE FIELD ACTIVITY 6
TEACHING AND TECHNOLOGY RUBRIC

After observing a teaching session by a teacher at the grade level or content area you would like to teach during which technology was used, mark the squares in the following rubric that best represent what you observed.

Evaluation Dimension	1 Poor	2 Average	3 Good	4 Excellent
Selection and incorporation of the technology into the lesson	The technology did not seem to fit with the lesson; It seemed disconnected for the method being used	The technology worked adequately in the context of the lesson and the method used	The technology selected supported the lesson and its use fit smoothly with the method used	The technology selected was ideal for this lesson and worked well to enhance the method
Skillful use of the technology	The teacher seemed to have difficulty using the technology; the lesson was interrupted by its use	The teacher seemed to know how to adequately use the technology	The teacher used the technology with ease; The lesson proceeded smoothly while using it	The teacher demonstrated mastery with the technology; the lesson was enhanced
Suitability of the technology to the students	The technology used did not seem to be at the student's level; Students were not engaged during use	The technology adequately engaged the students and appeared to be at their level	The technology engaged and interested the students; Students seemed interested when it was used	The technology clearly interested and engaged the students; They were active and involved during use
Technology accessible or viewable to all students	The technology used was not adequately viewable and/or accessible to all the students	The technology used could be seen and/or used by students with little difficulties	The technology used was easily seen by all students and could be accessed easily	The technology used was arranged so that all students could see and participate and were encouraged to do so
Up-to-date and working technologies	Only some of the technologies used were fully functional and working properly	Most of the technologies used were functioning and working as planned	Many of the technologies used were functional and working as intended	All of the technologies used worked well and as intended
Relevance of technology to the lesson objectives	Selection and use of this technology did not seem to be related to the lesson and its objectives	Selection and use of this technology adequately matched the lesson and objectives	This technology was appropriate to the lesson and to support the lesson's objectives	This technology was ideal for this lesson and it well supported the objectives
Technology met diverse learner needs	The technology did not seem to support the needs of diverse learning styles	The technology used supported some but not all learning styles	The technology used supported a majority of the learning styles of the students	The technology used offered support to all types of learning styles
TOTALS Add the values for the squares you marked in each column				

What overall rating do you feel is appropriate for the technology integration you observed? Justify your rating.

IN THE FIELD ACTIVITY 7
TEACHING AND LEARNING WITH TECHNOLOGY REFLECTION

You have observed and talked to a number of educators and administrators about educational technology and its use in the classroom and in schools. Consider what you saw and what you have learned. Respond fully to the following open-ended questions.

After thinking about what I saw or learned about educational technology in the classroom or the school, when I teach I want to remember to . . .

After seeing technology in action in the classroom and the school, I am convinced that . . .

After this experience, I believe that technology in teaching and learning is . . .

Post-test: Complete the following to determine your post-course level of educational technology competency. Circle the best answer from the choices provided.

1. A person's learning style influences how he or she best receives information.
   A. True   B. False

2. A theorist that is well known for seeing learning from a constructivist perspective is:
   A. B. F. Skinner   B. Howard Gardner
   C. Jean Piaget   D. Lev Vygotsky

3. The highest level of cognition in Bloom's Taxonomy is:
   A. Synthesis   B. Analysis
   C. Application   D. Evaluation

4. Instructional design is needed only when a very complex topic is being taught or when there are many students in the class.   A. True B.   False

5. A pixel refers to a single colored dot that, when combined with other dots, forms an image. The more pixels per inch, the better the image is.   A. True B.   False

6. A collection of computers and peripherals connected together to share information and resources is a:
   A. wireless device   B. network
   C. multimedia computer   D. expert system

7. Peripherals are hardware devices that are connected to a computer system.
                                                    A. True   B. False

8. A device that lets teachers display computer images using a standard television monitor is a:
   A.webcam   B. PDA
   C.scanner   D. scan converter

9. Productivity software typically does NOT include which of the following:
   A. electronic spreadsheet   B. authoring systems
   C. database management   D. word processing

10. Presentation software is often used in business applications but is seldom used in the classroom.
                                                    A. True   B. False

11. If a teacher needs to prepare an invitation for parents to attend the school's Open House, a possible software program would be:
    A. Drill-and-practice   B. Concept mapping
    C. Desktop publishing   D. Communications

12. Software that includes clip art libraries and enables one to draw, paint, and manipulate objects is known as graphics software.   A. True B.   False

13. To connect a computer to the Internet may require the following peripheral:
    A. portal   B. modem

C. search engine   D. newsgroup

14. Synchronous communication requires that two or more individuals be available at the same time.
                                        A. True   B. False

15. A problem with test generators is that they only select random questions, not allowing the teacher to select specific questions when needed.
                                        A. True   B. False

16. When a busy teacher finds a useful web site, a good way to be able to find it again is to:
    A. print out the page and file it   B. store it in Bookmarks or Favorites
    C. copy the link into a the class web site D. copy the URL on a sheet of paper

17. Compressed files are needed because digitized video files are large and take a long time to transmit across the Internet.
                                        A. True   B. False

18. Modern, up-to-date schools only use digital audio and video technologies in the classroom.
                                        A. True   B. False

19. Visual literacy is usually learned:
    A. in pre-school   B. in art classes
    C. by visual learners only   D. through many teaching and learning processes

20. Screening is often used to determine whether students' learning styles and study habits are such that they may be successful in a distance education format
                                        A. True   B. False

21. Interactivity between students in distance education may occur with all of the following except:
    A. email   B. assessments
    C. discussions   D. chats

22. The digital divide relates to inequity of access to technology
                                        A. True   B. False

23. Piracy occurs when:
    A. a student's information is posted on the Web without the parents' permission
    B. students in poor schools do not have access to technology
    C. software is installed in multiple computers but only one copy is purchased
    D. artificial intelligence systems are used in the classroom

24. Filtering software, which does not allow connection to unacceptable Internet sites, is necessary in school computers.   A. True   B. False

25. Which of the following is NOT a method for in-service teachers to access technology training?
    A. workshops   B. college and university courses
    C. vendor training   D. all of the above are acceptable methods

NOTES

NOTES

NOTES

NOTES

NOTES

NOTES

NOTES

NOTES

NOTES

NOTES